MIDNIGHT LIGHTS PUBLISHING HOUSE

PRESENTS:

BEE BEST APIARIST

AUTHOR OF THE BOOK:

BILL POLLIN

TABLE OF CONTENTS

COPYRIGHT © 2024 BY BILL POLLIN
ALL RIGHTS RESERVED.
NO PORTION OF THIS BOOK MAY BE REPRODUCED IN ANY
FORM WITHOUT WRITTEN PERMISSION FROM THE
PUBLISHER OR AUTHOR, EXCEPT AS PERMITTED BY U.S.
COPYRIGHT LAW.

Introduction

History of beekeeping

Beekeeping has been around for a very long time. Our ancestors started by stealing honey from wild bees. There are paintings in Spain that are 8,000 years old of people climbing cliffs to get honey. This dangerous practice slowly gave way to more managed approaches as early humans learned to coax swarms into hollow logs or clay pots.

Ancient Egyptians were among the first to develop sophisticated beekeeping techniques. They crafted cylindrical hives from clay and floated them down the Nile. The Greeks and Romans made beekeeping even better. Aristotle wrote about bees. In medieval Europe, monks made mead from honey.

In the 18th and 19th centuries, beekeeping changed a lot. In 1852, Lorenzo Langstroth invented the movable-frame hive. This allowed beekeepers to inspect and manage their colonies without destroying the comb. This, along with a growing understanding of bee biology, laid the foundation for modern apiculture. Today, we tend our hives to collect honey, but we also connect with our ancestors and the natural world.

Importance of bees in ecosystems and agriculture

Bees are important to many ecosystems. As they fly from flower to flower, they help plants to reproduce. This is important for the reproduction of plants that produce food for us. Bees help maintain biodiversity in natural habitats, which helps many plant and animal species survive.

Bees are important in agriculture. Crops like almonds, apples, blueberries, and cucumbers need bees to produce fruit. Bees are worth billions of dollars to agriculture every year. As a beekeeper, I've seen how placing hives near flowering crops can increase yields. It's a win-win for farmers, beekeepers and consumers.

However, bees are in danger from losing their homes and being poisoned. The decline of bees has raised alarm bells. As beekeepers, we are on the front lines of conservation efforts. Every time I open a hive, I'm reminded that I'm contributing to the health of entire ecosystems.

Overview of modern beekeeping practices

Modern beekeeping is a mix of art and science, based on tradition but with new ideas. Our Langstroth hives have moveable frames that make it easy to look after the bees. These hives are usually made of wood, but some beekeepers use plastic or polystyrene for better insulation. Inside, we use wax foundation or plastic frames to help the bees build their comb.

A typical beekeeping year follows the natural cycle of the colony. In spring, we check for the queen and ensure the colony has enough food. We might also split strong colonies to prevent swarming or to increase our hive numbers. As flowers begin to bloom, we add boxes on top of the hive to give the bees space to store surplus honey.

In summer, we monitor for pests and diseases, particularly the Varroa mite. We also harvest honey.

In autumn, we prepare for winter. We make sure our colonies have enough honey to survive the winter, sometimes adding sugar syrup if they need it. We might combine weak colonies to help them survive and add insulation or windbreaks to protect the hives from bad weather.

In winter, the bees are inside their hives for warmth. But we still check the hives to make sure they haven't been damaged by storms or pests. It's also when many beekeepers fix their equipment and plan for the next season.

Throughout the year, many beekeepers employ technology to assist in hive management. Digital scales can track changes in hive weight, indicating nectar flow or when feeding might be necessary. Temperature and humidity sensors help monitor conditions inside the hive, while some advanced systems even use audio analysis to detect issues like queenlessness.

Despite these technological advances, successful beekeeping still relies heavily on observation and intuition. Every time I open a hive, I'm not just looking at the bees – I'm listening to their buzz, smelling the distinct odors of the hive, and feeling the mood of the colony. This hands-on approach, honed through years of experience, is what turns beekeeping from a hobby into a craft. It's a continuous learning process, with each season bringing new challenges and insights into the fascinating world of bees.

Essential equipment and safety considerations for beekeepers

As a beekeeper, I know how important it is to have the right equipment and safety gear. I'll show you the essentials every beekeeper needs.

First, let's talk about protective gear. A good bee suit protects you from stings. I prefer a full suit that covers me from head to toe. Some beekeepers just wear a jacket and veil, but I prefer full coverage for peace of mind when working with defensive colonies.

The veil is the most important piece of protective gear. Your face and neck are sensitive, and a sting here can be dangerous. I use a rounded veil that keeps the mesh away from my face. It's attached to my suit, so bees can't get in.

Don't forget your hands! You need beekeeping gloves. I use leather gloves that go up my arms, protecting me without losing dexterity. Some beekeepers prefer nitrile gloves for more sensitivity, especially when marking queens.

Footwear is important too. I wear boots that my suit can tuck into, to keep bees off my legs. Make sure they're comfortable and sturdy – you'll be on your feet a lot.

Next, let's look at hive tools. The basic hive tool is something I use every time I open a hive. It's a multi-purpose tool used for prying apart hive bodies, scraping away excess wax and propolis, and more. I always keep a couple in my kit.

A smoker helps calm the bees, making hive inspections easier and safer. I use one with a good-sized bellows and chamber, which allows for longer burn times. Pine needles, cardboard, or commercial smoker fuel all work well.

A good pair of frame grips is useful for frame manipulation, especially when the hive is full of honey and the frames are heavy. I use strong hive bodies, frames, and foundation. Choose durable wood or plastic from a good supplier. Keep extra equipment on hand in case you need to add a super or replace a damaged component.

For honey harvesting, you'll need an uncapping knife or fork and an extractor. If you're just starting out, you might be able to borrow an extractor from a local beekeeping association.

Don't forget the little things: a notebook for record-keeping, a queen marking kit, feeding equipment, and a first-aid kit. A good beekeeping book or subscription to a beekeeping journal can help you when you're not sure how to handle a situation.

Beekeeping is about understanding and working with the bees as well as having the right equipment. Learn about bee behaviour and colony management. Your equipment is there to support you, but your knowledge and experience are your most valuable tools.

Biology of bees

Bee anatomy and physiology

As a beekeeper, I've spent a lot of time studying bees and I'm excited to share what I've learned. It's a complex subject, but understanding it is important for beekeeping.

Let's start with bee anatomy and physiology. Honeybees have a head, thorax and abdomen. The head has complex eyes for movement and simple eyes for light. Their antennae are very sensitive. They can smell, touch, and even detect carbon dioxide.

The bee's mouth parts are specialised for their diet. They have a long proboscis for sipping nectar and mandibles for other tasks. Bees have glands that make royal jelly, which is important for queen larvae.

The thorax is where the bee moves. They have six legs, each with a special job. The front legs have antennae cleaners, while the back legs have pollen baskets for collecting and transporting pollen. The four wings attached to the thorax allow for their impressive flight.

The abdomen contains many vital organs, including the honey stomach for nectar storage, the ventriculus for digestion, and the sting apparatus. Worker bees also have wax-producing glands on their abdomen.

Life cycle of bees

Let's look at the life cycle of bees. It all starts with an egg laid by the queen in a cell of the comb. After three days, the egg hatches into a tiny larva. Worker bees feed the larvae royal jelly for the first few days, then they eat honey and pollen (unless it's a queen, in which case it keeps eating royal jelly).

After about a week, the larva is sealed in its cell to pupate. It changes a lot during this time. After about 12 days for workers (15 for drones, 8 for queens), an adult bee emerges from the cell.

Roles within the colony (queen, workers, drones)

The roles in the colony are fascinating. The queen isn't in charge. She lays eggs, up to 2,000 a day at peak times. She also makes pheromones that help the colony behave.

Most of the hive is made up of female worker bees. Their roles change as they get older. Young workers start as cleaners and nurses. As they get older, they might become comb builders, food storers, or guard bees. In the latter part of their 4-6 week lifespan, they become foragers.

Drones, the male bees, have one purpose: to mate with virgin queens from other colonies. They don't work in the hive and are usually ejected before winter.

Bee communication and behavior

Bee communication and behaviour is amazing. The waggle dance is a good example. Foragers dance to show where food is. The angle shows the sun, and the length shows distance.

Bees also communicate through pheromones. The queen's pheromones help the colony stay together and stop workers from reproducing. Alarm pheromones tell other bees when a bee stings.

Pollination process

Finally, bees pollinate flowers, which is important for bees and our ecosystems. As bees visit flowers to get food, they transfer pollen from one flower to another, which helps plants reproduce.

Bees are good pollinators for several reasons. Their hairy bodies pick up pollen. Many species focus on one type of flower at a time, which increases the likelihood of successful pollination. Additionally, they visit many flowers, increasing pollination opportunities.

Different bee species have different tongue lengths and body sizes, which helps them pollinate different types of flowers. This is why it's important to have different types of bees in the environment.

Understanding bee biology helps me as a beekeeper. It helps me anticipate the needs of my colonies, spot potential problems early, and work in harmony with the bees' natural behaviours. I'm still amazed every time I open a hive. These insects create complex societies.

Setting up a hive

Choose the right location

The site should be sunny as bees are more active and productive in the sun. Morning sunlight helps warm up the hive, encouraging the bees to start foraging sooner.

The location should also be protected from strong winds. Trees or shrubs can protect the hives from strong winds. Make sure the site is well-drained and not prone to flooding. Wet conditions can cause problems with the hive.

Bees need to be able to access flowers and clean water. They also need a water source that is easy to reach.

It is also important to consider how easy it is for you to get to the site.

Types of hives and their pros/cons

There are several types of beehives, each with different features and benefits.

The *Langstroth hive* is the most popular because it is easy to manage and extract honey from. It can be scaled up as the colony grows. However, Langstroth hives are heavy and require more effort to move and manage. They cost more because you need extra equipment like frames and foundation.

The *top-bar hive* is simpler with horizontal bars across the top where bees build their combs. This type of hive is easier for hobbyists and those interested in a more natural approach to beekeeping. It is easier to build and doesn't require heavy lifting. Top-bar hives are more challenging to manage because the comb is fragile and honey production is lower. Inspection and disease management are also more difficult.

The *Warre hive* is designed to mimic the natural nesting environment of bees. It consists of stacked boxes without frames, allowing bees to build comb naturally. This hive type requires less intervention, promoting a hands-off beekeeping style. The Warre hive is good for people who care more about the bees than the honey. But it's harder to manage and check because the combs aren't on frames. Harvesting the honey is also more difficult.

Assembling Your First Hive

Once you've chosen the type of hive and a suitable location, you can start assembling it. First, prepare the site. Make sure the ground is level and consider placing the hive on a stand to protect it from moisture and pests.

For a Langstroth hive, start by building the hive stand and bottom board. Then, put together the brood boxes and frames, making sure the frames fit snugly within the boxes. If you want, add a queen excluder, then the honey supers, which are the boxes where bees will store honey. Put an inner cover and a telescoping outer cover on top to protect the hive from the elements.

For a top-bar hive, build the hive body and put on the top bars. Make sure the hive has a secure lid to protect it from rain and predators. The hive should also have ventilation holes to keep air moving.

A Warre hive is made by stacking boxes with quilted covers and a roof. Each box must fit well to allow the bees to move around easily.

Once the hive is built, you can introduce the bees. You can get bees in packages, nucs (nucleus colonies), or by catching swarms. Each method has its advantages. Packages are easier to transport and usually come with a queen, but they take longer to establish.

Nucs come with a small, established colony and a laying queen, which can speed up the hive's development. Swarms, if captured successfully, can be an economical option, but are less predictable. For nucs, put the frames from the nuc box into your hive, keeping the order the same. With swarms, shake or brush the bees into the hive.

Make sure the bees have food and water and check the hive regularly to see if the queen is accepted and the colony is healthy. With the right care, your hive will thrive and start making honey.

Acquiring bees: packages vs. nucs vs. swarms

Packages

This is a common way to start a new hive. It includes a screened box with about 2-3 pounds of worker bees (about 10,000 bees) and a separate container with a mated queen. This is easy to transport and can be used anywhere.

Also, they let you introduce bees to a new hive.

But starting with a package has problems. The bees need time to settle in and accept the queen, which can sometimes cause problems. This method also needs careful handling to make sure the bees move from the package to the hive.

Nucs

Nucs are small, established bee colonies. They usually consist of 3-5 frames of bees, brood, honey, and a laying queen. One advantage of nucs is that they come with a functional, cohesive colony. This can lead to faster colony growth and stability compared to packages.

Nucs cost more than packages because they are more developed. They are also harder to get during certain seasons and from certain suppliers. But nucs are better for new beekeepers because they start faster and have higher success rates.

Swarms

Another way to get bees is to catch a swarm. This happens when a colony gets too big and the old queen leaves with some of the worker bees to start a new hive. Swarming bees are usually calm, so it's easy to catch them and put them in a new hive. This is a cheap way to get bees and is fun for the beekeeper.

Swarming is unpredictable and depends on luck. There is also a risk that the captured swarm may have diseases or pests. Additionally, ensuring the swarm adapts to a new hive requires careful management and monitoring.

Installing Bees in a New Hive

Installing a Package

Before you start, make sure your hive is ready for the new bees. Have sugar syrup ready to feed the bees as they adjust to their new environment.

When you receive your package of bees, remove the queen cage from the package. Check the queen is alive and healthy. If the cage has a cork, remove it and replace it with a candy plug. This lets the bees gradually release the queen, giving them time to accept her. Hang the queen cage between two frames, with the candy end facing down or sideways. This helps ensure the queen's safe release. Next, release the worker bees. Gently shake or pour the bees into the hive, making sure they spread evenly across the frames. Once the bees are in the hive, place the inner and top covers on.

Feed the bees by placing a feeder with sugar syrup near the entrance or within the hive. Check the hive over the next few days to make sure the queen has been released and the bees are settling in.

Installing a Nucleus Colony (Nuc)

To install a nuc, transfer frames from an established colony into your new hive. Ensure your hive is ready and all equipment is in place. Carefully transport the nuc to your hive location.

Open the nuc box and remove each frame, inspecting for the queen, brood, and honey stores. Put the frames in the new hive one by one, keeping them in the same order. Be careful not to damage the comb or hurt the bees. Once all the frames are in, add more frames if there is space.

Put the frames in the middle of the hive, making sure they are evenly spaced. Close the hive by putting the inner and outer covers on. Give the bees sugar syrup to help them adjust to their new home.

Installing a Swarm

To install a swarm, first make sure the hive is ready. Put the hive in the chosen spot and remove the cover. If you caught the swarm in a container, put the bees in the hive. You can shake the bees directly into the hive or gently shake the container over the open hive. Another method is to place the container in the hive and let the bees move out on their own. Make sure the queen is introduced along with the workers.

After transferring the bees, close the hive with the inner and outer covers. Place a feeder with sugar syrup near the entrance. Monitor the hive over the following days to check for queen acceptance and overall colony health.

If you install your bees carefully and give them what they need, they will thrive.

Hive Management and Maintenance

Seasonal Hive Management Tasks

Your bees need different care at different times of the year.

Spring: Bees become more active in spring, so it's a good time to check the hive. Look for signs of disease or pests, and make sure the queen is laying eggs. If the colony is strong, add supers to provide space for honey storage and to prevent swarming. Swarming is common in spring, so regularly inspect the hive and, if necessary, perform splits or other swarm prevention techniques.

Summer: During the summer, bees are at their most active, foraging and producing honey. Regular inspections are essential to monitor the hive's health and check for pests like Varroa mites. Ensure there is enough space for the colony to expand by adding more supers if needed. In hot areas, add ventilation to prevent overheating. Watch for signs of swarming and manage accordingly. Harvest honey, leaving enough for the bees.

In autumn, prepare the hive for winter. Remove unused supers to reduce the hive's size. Check the colony has enough honey to last through winter (about 60 pounds). If stores are low, feed bees sugar syrup. Treat for mites and other pests. Insulate and protect the hive from wind and pests.

In winter, bees cluster together to stay warm. You don't need to check the hive often, but do check for signs of moisture, pests or other issues. Clear the hive entrance of snow and debris. On warmer days, you might see bees taking cleansing flights, which is normal. Don't open the hive unless you have to, as this can disrupt the bees' ability to regulate temperature.

Hive inspections: what to look for

It is important to check your hive regularly to make sure it is healthy. During inspections, look for the queen, eggs, larvae and capped brood. A healthy queen will have a regular and dense brood pattern. If the brood pattern is uneven, it could be a sign of a problem with the queen or a disease like American foulbrood.

Assess the amount of honey and pollen stored in the hive. This is important for the colony's survival, especially heading into winter. Also, look for signs of diseases like foulbrood, nosema, or chalkbrood.

Check the hive for gaps or damage that could let in pests or cold air. Replace any old or damaged frames.

Feeding Bees When Necessary

If the bees don't have enough food, you can feed them. Here are some ways to do this:

Sugar syrup: This is a common food for bees, especially in spring and autumn. Use a 1:1 ratio of sugar to water in spring to encourage brood rearing and a 2:1 ratio in autumn to help bees build up their winter stores. Feeders can be placed inside, at the entrance or on top of the hive.

Pollen Substitutes: If natural pollen is scarce, providing pollen patties or other substitutes can help support brood rearing and overall hive health.

Fondant or Candy Boards: During the winter, when liquid feed can cause moisture problems, solid feeds like fondant or candy boards are useful. You can put these on the frames or above the inner cover.

Honey: Bees like their own honey best. If you have extra honey from a strong colony, share it with weaker hives. Put honey frames in the hive or provide it in a feeder.

Managing pests and diseases

Pests and diseases can harm bees. Varroa destructor mites are a big problem. They feed on bees and spread viruses. Beekeepers use chemicals to control them. These miticides must be used according to the manufacturer's instructions to prevent resistance and ensure the bees' safety.

Mechanical controls are another way to control Varroa mites. Techniques like removing and destroying drone brood can effectively reduce mite populations. An integrated pest management (IPM) approach controls Varroa mite infestations. This approach combines chemical treatments, mechanical controls, and the use of mite-resistant bee strains.

Small hive beetles also damage beehives. These beetles burrow into combs, destroy honey, and disturb the brood. Managing small hive beetles involves using traps and bait within the hive. These traps attract and catch the beetles, so there are fewer of them. Keeping the hives clean and making sure there is not too much space in the comb can also stop the beetles. In very bad cases, you can use chemical treatments like CheckMite+ strips, but you must be careful and follow the safety rules.

Wax moths can damage weak hives by eating wax, pollen and honey. The best way to protect your hive is to keep it strong and healthy. You can also use traps and freezing to control the wax moth population. Fumigation with Paradichlorobenzene (PDB) crystals is effective against wax moths, but it should never be used on honey frames.

Nosema disease affects the gut of bees and leads to colony weakening. Fumagillin is an effective treatment for Nosema infections, and it should be administered according to the recommended guidelines to prevent resistance. Cleaning and replacing old combs can reduce spore loads and improve hive hygiene. Feeding bees with a medicated syrup can help them get better and support colonies affected by Nosema.

Splitting Hives and Creating New Colonies

Splitting hives is an important part of beekeeping. It helps to manage the number of bees in a colony, stop them from swarming, and create new colonies. This process involves dividing a strong colony into two or more separate hives.

To start, prepare the new hive by making sure it is fully assembled and has frames and foundation. Find a strong colony that is healthy and has a lot of bees. During the split, find the queen in the original hive. If possible, put her in one of the new hives with some brood, honey and bees. This makes sure that both hives have what they need to survive.

Carefully move the frames from the original hive to the new hive, keeping the same arrangement to keep the colony's structure. Make sure that each new hive has an equal amount of brood, bees and food. After the split, watch both hives to make sure the bees are doing well and that new queens are raised and mated if needed.

Overwintering Techniques

It's important to prepare your hive for winter to help your bees survive the cold months. As autumn approaches, reduce the hive size by removing any unused supers. This helps the bees maintain the temperature. Check the colony to ensure it has enough honey to last through winter, typically around 60 pounds. If the stores are insufficient, feed the bees sugar syrup to help them build up their reserves. Treat the hive for mites and other pests before winter sets in, as infestations can be detrimental during the colder months. Insulate the hive to protect it from harsh weather conditions. Reducing the hive entrance stops cold air and pests getting in, but lets in enough air to prevent moisture building up inside.

Check the hive regularly during winter to make sure it's dry and free of snow and debris. On warmer days, you might see bees taking cleansing flights, which is normal. Don't open the hive unless you really have to, as this can disrupt the bees' ability to maintain their internal temperature.

Honey Production Process

Nectar Collection by Bees

Honey production starts with bees collecting nectar. Worker bees leave the hive to find flowers. They use their long tongues to get nectar from flowers. This nectar is the main ingredient for honey. The nectar is stored in the bee's crop, a stomach for carrying food. The bee also picks up pollen during this process, which it transfers to other flowers to help with pollination.

The bee then gives the nectar to the other bees in the hive through a process called trophallaxis. The bee regurgitates the nectar into another bee's mouth. House bees turn nectar into honey.

How Bees Make Honey

Bees make honey by turning nectar into honey. The bees store the nectar in the hexagonal wax cells of the hive. Fresh nectar is prone to fermentation, so bees need to reduce its moisture level. They do this by fanning their wings, which makes the nectar dry out.

As the water content goes down, the bees' salivary glands break down the nectar's complex sugars into simpler sugars like glucose and fructose. Invertase is an important enzyme in this process. Glucose oxidase helps honey fight bacteria by producing hydrogen peroxide and gluconic acid.

When the nectar thickens and reaches the right moisture level (about 17-18%), the bees add a thin layer of beeswax to the honeycomb cells. This seals the honey and lets it be stored for a long time.

When and how to harvest honey

Harvesting honey is a delicate process that requires careful timing and technique to ensure the health of the colony and the quality of the honey.

When to harvest: The best time to harvest honey is when the bees have capped the cells. This means the honey is fully ripe and has the right amount of moisture. If the honey is not capped, it may still be too wet, which makes it more likely to ferment. The main harvest is usually in late summer or early autumn.

Harvesting Process: Wear protective gear to harvest honey. Use a bee smoker to calm the bees. Gently take the frames of honey from the hive, brushing off any bees.

You can then use an extractor to spin the frames and get the honey out. Uncap the wax seals with a knife or fork. Put the frames in the extractor and spin them to get the honey out. Collect the honey from the extractor and strain it through a fine mesh.

Once extracted, the honey can be stored in sterilised jars or containers. Make sure the containers are airtight to stop moisture getting in, which can cause fermentation. Store the honey in a cool, dark place to keep it fresh.

It is important to leave enough honey in the hive for the bees to survive the winter. A healthy colony needs around 60 pounds of honey, depending on the climate. By following these steps, you can harvest honey and keep your bees healthy.

Extracting and processing honey

Extracting and processing honey is a rewarding part of beekeeping. It transforms the hard work of your bees into a delicious and valuable product. The process involves several steps to ensure the honey is harvested and prepared properly.

Extracting Honey

When your hive frames are full of honey, it's time to extract. Put on protective clothing and use a bee smoker to calm the bees. Take the frames of honey from the hive, brushing off any bees.

Uncapping the honeycombs: First, remove the wax caps that seal the honey in the combs. You can use an uncapping knife or fork. Carefully remove the wax caps, taking care not to damage the comb.

Use a honey extractor. Put the uncapped frames in the extractor.

Extractors come in manual or electric versions and use centrifugal force to spin the honey out of the combs. Put the frames in the extractor and spin it according to the instructions. The honey will flow out of the extractor and into a container. Filter it through a fine mesh to remove any bits of wax or debris. This ensures the honey is clean and ready for storage.

Processing Honey

Honey needs minimal processing to be ready for consumption or sale. However, there are a few key steps to consider.

Heating (optional): Some beekeepers heat the honey to make it easier to filter and to delay crystallisation. However, excessive heating can degrade the honey's quality and nutritional value. If you choose to heat your honey, do so at a low temperature, ideally below 104°F (40°C).

Creamed honey is a popular product with a smooth, spreadable consistency. To make it, you control the crystallization process by introducing fine honey crystals and stirring until it thickens. Store it at a cool temperature to maintain its creamy texture.

Storing and Preserving Honey

Honey keeps well if you store it correctly. It is naturally resistant to spoilage, but it still needs to be handled properly.

Storage Containers: Store honey in clean, airtight containers to prevent it from absorbing moisture and odours from the environment. Glass jars are ideal, but food-grade plastic containers can also be used. Make sure the containers are thoroughly sterilised before use.

Storage Conditions: Keep honey in a cool, dark place, such as a pantry or cupboard. The ideal storage temperature is between 50-70°F (10-21°C). Avoid exposing honey to direct sunlight or storing it near heat sources, as this can cause it to darken and lose its flavour.

Preventing Crystallisation: Over time, honey naturally crystallises, forming granules. This doesn't affect the honey's quality, but it can change its texture. To slow crystallisation, store honey at a consistent, cool temperature. If your honey does crystallise, you can warm it gently in a water bath (not exceeding 104°F or 40°C) to return it to a liquid state.

Long-Term Preservation: Honey is known for its long shelf life and can last indefinitely if stored properly. Ancient honey in Egyptian tombs was still edible after thousands of years. To keep your honey in good condition, always seal containers tightly after each use and avoid moisture or contaminants.

Specialized Honey Production Techniques

Creamed Honey Production

Creamed honey is a type of honey that has been whipped. Creamed honey is a popular product known for its smooth consistency. Creamed honey doesn't drip and is easy to spread. The smooth texture is achieved by controlling the formation of crystals.

How is creamed honey made? To make good creamed honey, you need to control how it crystallises. Seed honey is used as a starter for the rest of the batch. A small amount of seed honey is mixed with liquid honey in a ratio of about 1:10. The mixture is stored at a cool temperature (around 14°C) to help the crystals form. Stir the honey now and then to make sure the crystals are spread evenly and don't get too big.

You will need the following equipment and tools: To make creamed honey, beekeepers need a honey mixer, temperature-controlled storage and seed honey. The honey mixer makes sure the seed honey is spread evenly through the batch, while the temperature-controlled storage units keep the right conditions for crystallisation. Use clean, sterilised containers to prevent contamination and preserve the honey's quality.

To get a smooth, consistent texture in creamed honey, you need to pay attention to detail and follow best practices. Start with high-quality, filtered liquid honey to avoid impurities that can affect the crystallization process. Monitor the temperature and stir the honey during crystallization to ensure a uniform texture. Using a high-quality seed honey with the desired texture can also affect the final product. Store the creamed honey in a cool, dry place to keep it consistent.

Infused Honey Production

What is infused honey? Infused honey is made by adding natural flavours to honey. This makes the honey taste and smell better, so it's a good ingredient for cooking and a favourite of food lovers.

Choose flavours: Choose high-quality, natural ingredients when making infused honey. Common infusions are cinnamon, vanilla, lavender, rosemary and citrus. The flavours should go well with the honey.

Infusion techniques: There are two ways to infuse honey: cold infusion and gentle heating. In cold infusion, you add the ingredients to the honey and let it steep for a few days. This method keeps the honey's natural qualities. Another way is to heat the honey to around 100°F (38°C) and add the flavouring. The honey is left to infuse for a few hours to a couple of days before straining out the solids.

Safety and Quality Control: Ensure the safety and quality of infused honey by using clean, sterilised containers and high-quality ingredients. Avoid adding moisture to the honey as this can cause fermentation and spoilage. After infusion, strain the honey and store it in an airtight container in a cool, dark place.

Honeycomb Honey Production

Honeycomb honey is honey that is sold in the beeswax cells that bees produce. This type of honey is highly prized for its pure, unprocessed state and the natural texture provided by the wax comb. One common method is using Ross Rounds or section frames, which allow bees to build honeycomb in small, individual sections that can be easily harvested and packaged. Another traditional method involves using shallow frames and cutting the comb into squares once the honey is fully capped.

Harvesting and Packaging: Harvesting comb honey involves removing the frames from the hive when the honey is fully capped. The frames are then cut into sections or removed as whole rounds. The honeycomb is often placed in clear containers to show off its natural beauty. It must be kept intact during harvesting and packaging to keep its quality and appearance.

Market and Consumer Preferences: Comb honey appeals to consumers looking for a natural, unprocessed product. It can be marketed as a gourmet item, emphasizing its purity and unique eating experience. Comb honey is often enjoyed on its own, spread on toast, or used as a topping for desserts and cheeses.

Single-Origin Honey Production

Single-origin honey is honey from a specific place. Single-origin honey is from one place and has a unique taste, colour and smell. This type of honey shows the taste of the soil, like fine wine, and is liked by connoisseurs and chefs.

Managing Forage Areas: Beekeepers must place hives in areas with lots of specific flowers to produce single-origin honey. Beekeepers must make sure that the plants in the forage areas are the main source of nectar during the honey flow period. This may mean choosing places where bees are less likely to forage on other plants.

Seasonal considerations: Timing is important for single-origin honey.

Beekeepers must harvest the honey right after the target plants bloom to keep it pure. This often requires careful planning and monitoring of local plant blooming cycles.

Marketing single-origin honey: single-origin honey can be marketed by emphasising its unique flavour profile and the specific region it comes from. Labels should highlight the floral source and geographic origin, appealing to consumers interested in high-quality, artisanal products. Storytelling about the region and the beekeeping practices can enhance the product's appeal.

Organic Honey Production

Organic honey is free from pesticides, chemicals, and antibiotics. Bees, plants and hive management must comply with organic standards set by regulators.

Organic beekeeping: Organic beekeeping is about keeping bees in a healthy way. This means keeping apiaries away from conventional farming and pollution, using organic treatments for pests and diseases, and making sure bees have access to pesticide-free food.

Challenges and Solutions: Producing organic honey is hard because you have to find a good place and keep up organic practices throughout the process. Solutions include working with organic farms, creating buffer zones around apiaries, and using natural methods to control pests and diseases. Beekeepers must keep detailed records to demonstrate compliance with organic standards.

Market Trends: There is a growing demand for organic products as consumers become more health-conscious and environmentally aware. Organic honey appeals to this market, and beekeepers can command higher prices for certified organic products. Marketing strategies should focus on the health and environmental benefits of organic honey.

Raw Honey Production

Raw honey is honey that has not been heated or processed. It is typically strained to remove larger particles but retains its natural pollen and beneficial compounds.

Quality control: To keep raw honey pure and good, beekeepers must handle it carefully to avoid contamination. They should use clean, sterilised equipment and store honey in airtight containers to prevent moisture absorption and spoilage. Regular testing for moisture content and other quality parameters can help maintain high standards.

Consumer education: To market raw honey, beekeepers must educate consumers about its natural enzymes, antioxidants, and health benefits.

Fair Trade Honey Production

Fair trade honey is produced in a way that ensures fair wages and working conditions for beekeepers, along with environmentally sustainable practices. Fair trade certification aims to support small-scale beekeepers and promote ethical sourcing.

Certification Process: Beekeepers and honey producers must work with certifying organisations to undergo audits and demonstrate compliance with fair trade criteria.

Beekeepers benefit from fair trade honey programs. These programs provide fair prices and access to international markets. They also support community development projects, training, and resources to improve beekeeping practices.

Marketing fair trade honey involves emphasizing its ethical and sustainable production methods. Labels should highlight the fair trade certification, and storytelling about the beekeepers and their communities can enhance the product's appeal.

Honey Blends Production

Honey blends are made from different types of honey. This makes them consistent, enhances specific qualities, and balances the natural variations in honey production.

To make honey blends, different types of honey are mixed in precise proportions to achieve the desired flavour, colour, and consistency. Beekeepers and producers need to know the properties of each honey type they use. For example, a blend might combine clover honey with buckwheat honey to create a balanced product.

The blending process can be done manually or with the help of specialised mixing equipment. Manually blending honey involves measuring and mixing different honeys in batches. Honey is combined in large vats or tanks with a mixer to ensure even distribution of flavors and consistency.

It is important to test the honey for moisture content, sugar composition, and impurities to ensure the final product meets the desired specifications.

Quality assurance also involves keeping records of where the honey comes from and how much of each type is used in each blend. This transparency helps producers to make sure they can make the same blends again and again. By noting down what each batch is like, producers can make changes to future blends to get the best results.

Blended honey is used in many different ways, making it a useful product for consumers and the food industry. Blended honey is often sold in shops because it tastes the same every time and is reliable. Blended honey comes in different forms, like jars, squeeze bottles, and single-serve packets.

Chefs and food manufacturers use blended honey to create consistent flavors in recipes and food products. It is used in baked goods, sauces, marinades and drinks to enhance the flavour. Blended honey is used to make special food items like honey spreads and infused honeys.

Blending honey helps sustain beekeeping by using honey from different regions and flowers, reducing pressure on any one place. This helps local ecosystems by encouraging different types of bees to forage.

Blending honey can also help with the impact of seasonal and environmental changes on honey production. By combining honey from different sources, producers can ensure a stable supply of high-quality honey, even in years when certain floral sources may be less abundant.

It is important to educate consumers about the benefits and characteristics of blended honey. This helps them appreciate and demand the product. Highlighting the careful selection and blending process, as well as the sensory qualities of the final product, can help differentiate blended honey from single-source varieties. Providing information about the sustainability and environmental benefits of blending honey can also enhance its appeal to eco-conscious consumers.

Types of Honey and Their Properties

Honey comes in different types, each with its own properties. Knowing these types helps us appreciate the diversity of honey.

Monofloral honey

Monofloral honey is made from one type of flower. This makes the honey taste, look and feel different.

Acacia honey: Acacia honey is light and sweet. It stays liquid for a long time because it has a lot of fructose, so it doesn't crystallise. It is clear and tastes subtle, so it is a favourite for cooking and as a sweetener in tea and desserts.

Manuka honey: This honey is produced in New Zealand from the Manuka tree and is known for its medicinal properties. It is dark and bitter. Manuka honey contains special compounds like methylglyoxal (MGO) that make it antibacterial. It is used for healing wounds and improving digestion.

Lavender honey: This honey has a floral aroma and a light amber colour. Lavender honey is popular because of its unique flavour, which goes well with cheese and baked goods. It is also used in natural remedies.

Buckwheat honey: Buckwheat honey is dark and strong, with a molasses-like flavour. It is rich in antioxidants and is often used in baking or as a cough suppressant. The dark colour indicates a high mineral content.

Orange blossom honey is light, citrusy and pale amber. It is fragrant and sweet, making it ideal for salad dressings, marinades and desserts.

Clover honey is light and mild. It can be used in many ways, from sweetening drinks to baking.

Eucalyptus honey is dark and has a minty flavour. It is used for its medicinal properties, particularly for respiratory issues.

Polyfloral honey

Polyfloral honey is made from the nectar of different flowers. It has a more complex flavour than other types of honey.

Wildflower Honey: The taste, colour and smell of wildflower honey can vary a lot depending on where it is collected. It is usually very sweet and strong-tasting, with a flavour that reflects the different flowers that the bees visit. Wildflower honey is often used in teas, on toast and in baking.

Forest Honey: Collected from mixed forest environments, this honey can taste quite complex, with hints of different wildflowers, herbs and even tree sap. It is usually darker and richer than meadow honey and is very flavourful.

Mountain Honey: Bees that live in mountains make honey that tastes of the flowers and herbs they find there.

Meadow Honey: Bees that live in meadows make honey that tastes of the flowers and grasses they find there.

Medicinal properties of different honeys

Honey has been used for medicinal purposes for centuries. Different types of honey offer various health benefits.

Manuka honey is produced from the nectar of the Manuka tree in New Zealand. It is renowned for its strong antibacterial and antimicrobial properties. Manuka honey has high levels of methylglyoxal (MGO), which makes it good for wound healing, reducing infection and promoting skin health. It is also good for sore throats, digestive health and immunity.

Buckwheat honey is rich in antioxidants, which help to neutralise free radicals and reduce oxidative stress. This dark honey is good for soothing coughs and sore throats due to its high phenolic content. Its antioxidant properties support immune function and overall health.

Eucalyptus honey is antiseptic and anti-inflammatory. It is used to relieve colds and respiratory issues. The menthol-like flavour of eucalyptus honey is soothing, making it a popular choice in natural remedies for respiratory health.

Lavender honey is calming and anti-inflammatory. It can be used to treat minor burns and wounds. It is also used in aromatherapy and natural remedies to reduce anxiety, promote relaxation, and improve sleep quality.

Tualang honey is harvested from the Tualang tree in Southeast Asia. It is known for its high antioxidant content and various medicinal properties. It is used in traditional medicine to treat wounds, enhance skin health, and boost the immune system. Studies have shown that Tualang honey has anti-inflammatory, antimicrobial, and wound-healing properties.

Grading and Quality Standards for Honey

Honey quality and grading standards are essential to ensure that consumers receive a product that meets specific criteria for purity, taste, and safety. Various organisations and regulations govern these standards, focusing on aspects such as moisture content, purity, and adulteration. The ideal moisture content for honey is below 18%. Beekeepers and honey producers use refractometers to measure and ensure the appropriate moisture content. Pure honey should not contain any additives or adulterants. Common adulterants include sugar syrups, corn syrup, and other sweeteners. Authentic honey maintains its natural composition without dilution or enhancement. To test for purity, honey is analysed for its sugar profile, foreign substances and pollen content.

Honey is graded in different countries based on colour, clarity, flavour and aroma. In the United States, honey is graded by the USDA into four grades: Grade A, Grade B, Grade C and Substandard. Grade A honey is the best quality. Other countries have similar grading systems for honey.

Pollen analysis can help identify the honey's quality and origin. High-quality honey should contain a diverse pollen profile.

Crystallization and Decrystallization of Honey

Crystallization

Honey can form crystals when it is heated or cooled. This does not affect the honey's quality, but it can change how it looks and feels. The main thing that affects this is the amount of glucose and fructose in the honey. Honey with more glucose in it tends to crystallise faster because glucose is less soluble in water than fructose. For example, clover and sunflower honeys crystallise more quickly than acacia or tupelo honeys. Temperature also affects crystallisation. Honey stored at cooler temperatures (between 50-59°F or 10-15°C) crystallises more quickly than honey stored at higher temperatures. This is because lower temperatures make it easier for glucose to form crystals. How you store honey affects how quickly it crystallises. Honey stored in a cool, dark place with little change in temperature is less likely to crystallise quickly than honey stored in an area with big temperature changes.

To keep honey from crystallising, store it in a dark, dry place at temperatures above 64°F (18°C). Creamed honey is intentionally crystallised to have a smooth, spreadable consistency. This is achieved by controlling the crystallisation process. Creamed honey is smooth and doesn't crystallise.

Airtight containers stop moisture getting in, which can cause honey to crystallise. Glass jars are best for long-term storage as they don't let in moisture or odours.

Decrystallization

Honey can be returned to a liquid state by heating it gently. This process, called decrystallisation, is important for preserving honey's quality and nutritional value. One way to do this is to place the jar in a warm water bath. The water should not exceed 104°F (40°C) to avoid damaging the honey's enzymes and compounds. Stirring the honey helps distribute the heat and speeds up the process.

Don't use a microwave to decrystallise honey. Microwaves can overheat the honey, which breaks down the enzymes and loses the honey's nutritional value.

To keep honey from crystallising again, store it properly. Use clean, airtight containers and keep it at a stable, warm temperature.

Other bee products

Beeswax: Harvesting, Processing, and Uses

Beeswax is made by honeybees to build their honeycombs. Beeswax is harvested by removing wax cappings from honeycomb cells during honey extraction. Beekeepers collect the cappings and old combs. The wax is melted in a double boiler to prevent it from overheating. The wax is filtered to remove impurities. The wax is then cooled and hardens. This process can be repeated to make the beeswax even purer.

Processed beeswax is very useful. It is used in candles, where it makes candles burn longer and cleaner than those made from paraffin. Beeswax is used in cosmetics, food preservation, and art. It is a natural moisturizer and protector.

Propolis: Collection and Health Benefits

Propolis is a resin collected by bees from tree buds and sap flows. Bees use it to seal gaps in the hive and reinforce its structure. Beekeepers collect it by scraping it from hive parts or using special traps. These traps are placed in the hive and removed once filled with propolis, which is then chilled to harden and easily scraped off.

Propolis has health benefits, including antimicrobial, anti-inflammatory, and antioxidant properties. It is used to treat minor wounds and infections due to its natural antibiotic qualities. Propolis can reduce inflammation and promote healing, making it useful for treating skin conditions like eczema and psoriasis. It also helps the immune system and is found in many natural health products for boosting immunity and oral health, such as toothpaste and mouthwash.

Royal Jelly: Production and Applications

Royal jelly is a sweet, sticky substance made by worker bees to feed larvae and the queen. Royal jelly is a substance made by worker bees to feed larvae and the queen bee. It is made by nurse bees. Beekeepers collect royal jelly by encouraging the production of queen cells, which are then harvested before the larvae can eat it.

Royal jelly is good for your health. It is a dietary supplement because it contains vitamins, minerals, and amino acids. These are believed to boost energy, enhance immunity, and improve overall health. Royal jelly is used in anti-ageing creams and lotions because it makes skin look younger. Royal jelly can lower cholesterol, reduce inflammation, and support wound healing.

Bee Pollen: Harvesting and Nutritional Value

Bee pollen is collected by bees from flowers and packed into granules with nectar and enzymes. Beekeepers use traps at the hive entrance to collect pollen from bees on their way back from foraging. The traps collect pollen from the bees' legs, which is then harvested.

Bee pollen is a superfood. It contains all the essential amino acids, making it a complete protein source. It is also packed with vitamins and minerals. The antioxidants help combat stress and support overall health. Bee pollen can enhance the immune system and is used to treat allergies and boost energy levels.

Bee Venom: Collection and Therapeutic Uses

Bee venom is collected from bees using a special device. The venom is put on a glass plate and left to dry. This process is designed to ensure that the bees do not die after stinging. It contains melittin, which is anti-inflammatory, useful for arthritis and chronic pain. Bee venom can also modulate the immune system, offering potential for autoimmune diseases such as multiple sclerosis. In skincare, bee venom is included in anti-aging products due to its ability to stimulate collagen production and improve skin elasticity. Some studies also suggest that bee venom therapy may support neurological health and improve symptoms in conditions such as Parkinson's disease.

Common challenges and solutions

Dealing with Aggressive Bees

Aggressive bees can be a challenge for beekeepers. One way to manage them is to requeen the colony with a gentler queen. This can change the colony's temperament over time. It's important to get queens from reliable breeders. Another approach is to keep the hive in good condition and not disturb it too much. Regular, gentle inspections can help. Using a smoker can calm the bees, making them less likely to sting. Beekeepers should also make sure their gear is good, as this makes them more confident and less likely to move quickly, which can make the bees more aggressive.

The environment can also affect bee behaviour. If bees have lots of food and clean water, they are less likely to fight. It is also good to put hives somewhere quiet and away from busy roads.

Inspecting hives on mild, sunny days can reduce the number of bees in the hive and their defensive behaviour. Understanding and avoiding triggers for bee aggression can make interactions with the hive smoother.

Preventing and Managing Swarming

Swarming is a natural process for bees, but it can result in the loss of a significant portion of the colony. To prevent swarming, beekeepers should regularly monitor the hive during peak swarming seasons (spring and early summer) and provide enough space for the colony to expand. Adding supers (additional hive boxes) can help alleviate congestion within the hive.

Beekeepers should regularly inspect their hives to identify early signs of swarming, such as the presence of swarm cells. If swarm cells are detected, they can perform a controlled split of the hive, creating a new colony with some of the bees and brood. This mimics the natural swarming process but allows the beekeeper to retain control. Another method to prevent swarming is to requeen the hive periodically. Young queens are less likely to swarm. Requeening every one to two years can help maintain a stable colony. Ensure the hive has good ventilation and is not overheated to reduce the likelihood of swarming.

Provide sufficient forage and manage the hive's nutritional needs. When bees have abundant resources and the hive is well-fed, they are less inclined to swarm. Beekeepers can remove old combs to keep bees in the hive. If a swarm does happen, beekeepers should be ready to catch it and put it back in the hive. Setting up bait hives with old comb and pheromone lures can help catch swarms. This helps bees that swarm to be recaptured and managed.

Recognizing and Treating Common Bee Diseases

Bees can get sick. This can hurt the colony and make it less productive. One common disease is caused by a mite called Varroa destructor. Beekeepers should check for mites often. If there are many, they can use a mite treatment called Apivar or Apiguard.

Another disease is American Foulbrood (AFB), which affects bee larvae. AFB is highly contagious and can be devastating to colonies. Symptoms include sunken, perforated brood caps and a foul odor. Beekeepers should immediately quarantine affected hives and burn infected equipment. Antibiotics can be used as a preventive measure, but strict management practices are crucial to control the spread.

Nosema is a disease caused by parasites that affect the digestive system of bees. It can weaken colonies and cause symptoms like dysentery and reduced hive activity. Fumagillin is an effective treatment for Nosema. Maintaining hive hygiene and replacing old comb can also help prevent the disease. This disease often arises from poor ventilation and damp conditions within the hive. Improving ventilation and maintaining hygiene can help prevent chalkbrood. Removing and destroying affected brood combs can also control its spread. Beekeepers should also try to keep their bees from getting the same virus twice.

Protecting Hives from Predators

Predators like bears, skunks, raccoons and birds can harm bee colonies. Electric fences can keep larger predators like bears away. The fence should be set up before bears become a problem. It is easier to prevent bears from getting into the hives than to stop them once they have tasted the honey.

For smaller predators like skunks and raccoons, raising hives off the ground can prevent these animals from reaching the hive entrance. Additionally, placing rough materials like chicken wire or nails around the hive stands can discourage these predators from climbing.

Birds, particularly bee-eaters, can also pose a threat. Positioning hives in areas with ample cover or using bird deterrents can help protect bees. A physical barrier around the apiary can also help.

Wasps and hornets can invade hives and kill bees. Reducing wasp nests and using traps can help control these predators. Ensuring that hive entrances are the right size can also prevent larger predators from entering the hive.

A clean and orderly apiary is less attractive to predators. Remove food sources and waste regularly. Monitor hives for signs of predation and take action if you find evidence of predators.

Addressing Colony Collapse Disorder (CCD)

Colony Collapse Disorder (CCD) is when most worker bees in a colony disappear, leaving the queen, brood, and a few nurse bees. The exact cause of CCD is not known, but it is believed to result from a combination of factors, including pesticide exposure, pathogens, poor nutrition, and environmental stressors.

To address CCD, beekeepers should adopt integrated pest management (IPM) practices to control Varroa mites and other pests without over-relying on chemical treatments. This approach includes regular monitoring, using biological controls, and rotating chemical treatments to prevent resistance.

Ensuring that bees have access to diverse and abundant forage is crucial. Planting a variety of nectar- and pollen-rich plants around the apiary can improve bee nutrition and resilience. If there is not enough food, bees can be given extra food to help them stay healthy. Replacing old comb and cleaning hive equipment can help to reduce disease.

Promoting diversity in bee populations can help bees to cope with stress. By addressing these factors, beekeepers can help to reduce the risk of CCD and support the health of their colonies.

Environmental impact and conservation

The Role of Bees in Biodiversity

Bees are important for biodiversity. They help plants to reproduce, including many food crops. About 75% of global food crops depend on bees and other insects for pollination. This includes fruits, vegetables, nuts, and seeds, which are important for human diets. Without bees, food crops would be less productive, which would make food more expensive for people.

Bees also help other plants to reproduce, which helps wildlife. This in turn helps to maintain soil, water and carbon in the environment.

Bees also help plants to reproduce in different ways. This makes plants more likely to survive and adapt to changing conditions.

In nature, bees help trees and shrubs to grow. Many trees and shrubs rely on bees for pollination, and their seeds are spread by animals that depend on bee-pollinated fruits and nuts. Bees depend on other creatures in the environment for their own survival. When bees die off, other creatures die too. This can make the environment less healthy.

Threats to Bee Populations

Bees are in danger. Their numbers are falling fast. Bees need flowers and nesting sites to survive. But these are being lost as cities grow, farms expand and forests are cut down. If landscapes are changed into one type of plant, bees don't get the food they need to survive.

Pesticides, particularly neonicotinoids, also harm bees. These chemicals are used in agriculture and affect bees' ability to forage, navigate, and reproduce. Studies have shown that exposure to neonicotinoids can impair bees' immune systems, making them more vulnerable to pathogens.

Climate change is affecting bees. Changes in temperature and rain affect the plants bees pollinate. Extreme weather can harm bees and their habitats. Climate change can also change where bees live, so they no longer have access to the flowers they need to survive.

Pathogens like the Varroa destructor mite and Nosema fungi harm bees. The Varroa mite is a big threat to honeybees. It eats bee larvae and adults and passes on viruses. If not managed, infestations can weaken colonies, reduce brood production and lead to colony collapse.

Pollution can also harm bees. Contaminated nectar and pollen can affect their health and reproductive success. Light pollution can disrupt their foraging patterns and navigation.

Creating Bee-Friendly Gardens and Habitats

Creating bee-friendly gardens and habitats helps bees and other insects.

Planting different types of flowers at different times of the year helps bees. Native plants are best because they have evolved with local bees.

A mix of plant types, including trees, shrubs, perennials, and annuals, creates a diverse and attractive habitat for bees. Flowering herbs, fruits, and vegetables can also be added to a bee-friendly garden. Plants such as lavender, sunflowers, clover, and wildflowers are great for attracting and supporting bees. Instead, use natural controls, such as introducing insects that prey on pests. If chemical treatments are necessary, choose bee-friendly options and apply them when bees are not active.

Providing nesting sites helps support solitary bees. You can create bee hotels by drilling holes in wood blocks or bundling hollow stems. This provides nesting habitats for species such as mason bees and leafcutter bees. You can also leave patches of bare ground and avoid excessive mulching to benefit ground-nesting bees.

Water sources are important for bees, especially during hot weather. A shallow dish filled with water and pebbles or marbles provides a safe place for bees to drink without drowning. Ensure the water is kept clean and replenished regularly.

If people work together to create and maintain spaces that are good for bees, it will have a bigger impact. If people learn about why bees are important and how they can help them, more people will start to do things that help bees. Community gardens, green spaces and conservation projects can help bees and the environment.

Impact of Pesticides on Bees

Pesticides are killing bees. Neonicotinoids are a type of pesticide that bees can't resist. They get into the plants and are in the nectar and pollen. Bees exposed to these chemicals can experience a range of sublethal effects, even if they don't die immediately.

Research shows that neonicotinoids can make bees less able to learn, remember and find their way back to the hive. This can lead to fewer bees foraging and weaker colonies. They can also make bees less efficient at collecting nectar and pollen.

Neonicotinoids can also make bees more vulnerable to diseases and parasites. Studies have shown that bees exposed to these chemicals have lower resistance to pathogens like Nosema and viruses transmitted by Varroa mites. This increased vulnerability can lead to higher mortality rates and colony collapse.

The use of pesticides can also disrupt ecosystems. By reducing bee populations, pesticide use can negatively impact plant pollination and the reproductive success of many plant species. This affects animals that eat these plants, which can have wider effects on the environment.

To help bees, countries have banned or restricted some neonicotinoids. Other ways to help bees are to use biological controls and less chemical pesticides. Farmers and gardeners can use bee-friendly practices, such as using targeted pesticides and less harmful alternatives.

If people know about pesticides and want to buy pesticide-free food, farmers will change how they work. Buying organic food helps reduce the use of pesticides and protects bees and other pollinators.

Conservation Efforts and How to Get Involved

Bees are important for the environment and agriculture. Conservation efforts are needed to protect them. Many organisations and initiatives are working to save the bees. You can help in many ways.

One way to help bees is to create and keep habitats that provide them with food, nesting sites and shelter. Growing bee-friendly gardens, helping with community gardening, and supporting local conservation can help create more bee-friendly environments.

Advocacy and education are also important for bee conservation. If people know more about bees and what is hurting them, they can help make new rules and get more support for conservation. This can include supporting campaigns to reduce pesticides, protect nature and promote sustainable farming.

Supporting research is important for bee conservation. Research helps us understand bee populations and find ways to conserve them. You can support research by donating to organisations that fund bee-related studies or by taking part in citizen science projects.

Local and national conservation organisations can help to protect bees. Many organisations offer volunteer opportunities, educational resources, and advocacy tools. Examples of such organisations include the Xerces Society for Invertebrate Conservation, the Pollinator Partnership, and local beekeeping associations.

Buying products that support sustainable practices can help bees. Choose organic and locally produced honey, support farmers who use bee-friendly practices, and avoid products treated with harmful pesticides.

By taking these actions, individuals can help conserve bees and ensure the sustainability of ecosystems and the availability of crops that depend on bee pollination.

www.ingramcontent.com/pod-product-compliance
Lightning Source LLC
Chambersburg PA
CBHW050828250726
48653CB00006B/2486